MY SOUL'S JOURNEY

W.C. ALDRIDGE

MY SOUL'S JOURNEY

collected poems

Worldwind Books  Albuquerque

copyright © 2021 by W.C. Aldridge

All rights reserved, including the right to reproduce this book or any part thereof, in any form, except for inclusion of brief quotes for a review.

Printed in the United States of America
First Printing, 2021
ISBN: 978-0-938513-71-1
Library of Congress Control Number: 2021938640

Cover and page 36: "5th Grade Substitute" by Annie Lee (1985, acrylic). Image used with permission and provided by the Annie Lee Art Foundation (AFL35.org).

Photographs pages 9, 44, 66, 81 and 90 © Michele Lee, Black Butterfly Photography-Chicago; used with permission.

WORLDWIND BOOKS
an imprint of
Amador Publishers, LLC
Albuquerque, New Mexico
www.amadorbooks.com

Dedications

TO: Mom and Daddy (Herbert): in memoriam of my otherworldly heroes, I love you dearly. Thank you for supporting me, always. Rest in Grace.

AND

TO: Reggie, Auntie Ronnie, Cly, Haniyyah, and Toni J: Thank you.

Acknowledgments

I thank you Lord Jesus for giving me the words to say. I acknowledge You.

Grateful acknowledgment is made to Abe Ilo, Director of the Annie Lee Art Foundation (AFL35) for arranging for the use of Annie Lee's artwork for this edition.

Grateful acknowledgment is also made to photographer Michele Lee, Black Butterfly Photography-Chicago, for providing the photographs for this edition.

I acknowledge Zelda Gatuskin and Amador Publishers, LLC along with Worldwind Books Poetry Series for bringing this work to fruition. Twice is the charm. I also acknowledge Sinead G. Kelley for working with me to piece together my life's details.

MY SOUL'S JOURNEY
Contents

Chapter 1 / Forgiveness Is Not a Byword
A Time to Release / 2
A Gift / 3
How is It / 4
I Choose to Forgive / 5

Chapter 2 / Inspiration
The Sky is My Floor / 8
When I Look Forward to the Backfire / 10
Light it Up! / 11

Chapter 3 / Dedications
Her Graduation (To C.R.P.) / 14
Here You are at 30 (To H.B.C.) / 15
And So There is Dorothy Mae (To D.M.Y. – Matriarch) / 18
He Knew How to Be a Father (To H.W.Y. – Patriarch) / 20
Joseph Does Rise (To Pastor E.A.B.) / 22
Situational Cancer (To the Innocent) / 24
Tired (Bully) / 26
Planted by the River (To the Joshua Generation) / 28
Ms. Perfection Says Goodbye (To We Girls and Women) / 31

Chapter 4 | Scriptures
Snowflake / 34
Ever Present / 37
Talent / 38
Act / 39

Chapter 5 / My Relationship with God
God is (...) *Good* / 42
What it's Like / 43
Dust / 46
Tears in Your Bottle / 48

Chapter 6 / Everything is about Color
Color Carries Feeling / 50
Mocha Chocolate-Skinned / 52

Chapter 7 / Observations, Reminiscences, Reflections
These are Kind of Like Thoughts / 56
Prisoner / 57
She Loved Me More / 58
T-I-S Tizzz / 59
Austin / 61
Chest Pain / 62
Opportunity / 63
Give / 64
Where I Grew (A Narrative Poem) / 65
Breakthrough / 73
Men Don't Leave / 74
Sundry Times / 76
Black Ink on My Fingers / 77
Same. Difference. / 79
Wall of Words / 82
Taking Away the Swiss Cheese / 83
Quiet Noise / 85
Process / 87
Wise Choice / 88
Dreams / 88
To Be and To Do / 89

Chapter 8 / I'm Not a Poor Frog
Heart Made Happy / 94
Never Thought / 96

Chapter 9 / For the Love of Ellipses…
Relationship… / 98
Grass is Grass (Things aren't always…well you know…) / 99

Chapter 10 / Peace and Peace's Intermission
Inside Peace / 102
Quiet. / 103
Broken Pieces / 104
Peace's Intermission / 105

About the Author / 107

List of Illustrations

"5th Grade Substitute" by Annie Lee / Cover and page 36
"Breakthrough" by Michele Lee / 9
"Scarlet Heart" by Michele Lee / 44
"Austin's Quiet Jubilee" by Michele Lee / 60
"Wise Eyes" by Michele Lee / 66
"Mr. and Mrs. Duck" by Michele Lee / 81
"Platform Walk" by Michele Lee / 84
"Solemn Solitude" by Michele Lee / 90
Portrait of W.C. Aldridge by Michele Lee / 106

Forgiveness Is Not a Byword

Chapter 1

A Time to Release

Carrying a burden upon her shoulder,
Walking through the grime and grit,
Not a lot and not a bit,
Time has passed, hence becomes a boulder.
It seems the baggage has gotten older,
Age does not matter, and she cannot sit,
Sweat and dirt have formed a clique,
Upon her brow, the heat has smoldered.
The stench of her soul has filled her senses,
To taste, to touch, and to see,
Has caused her very heart to flee,
To run than mend her broken fences.
Her spirit has then grown colder…
The weight grows heavier without sweet mercy.

A Gift

Being able to forgive…
Is a serious gift from God.
I say gift, because it seems such a daunting task,
Until God gives you the ability to do so…
By faith.
I wonder if that gift will be granted when
Anger flares up full force,
Coming at you like bullets with sparks flying
Straight to the heart, knife stabbing,
Heart palpitating pain that
Just doesn't seem to let up.

But then faith steps in
And causes the heart to calm,
The knife to seize,
The bullets to stop and the sparks to burn out…
I can then put my arms up and breathe freely,
Because I have freely received,
The gift of forgiving…
By faith.

In Jesus' name.
Amen.

How Is It

How is it,
That love and hate can dwell in the same being?
The conception of pain,
That comes forth in a word, nuance, or bitter gesture,
Not exactly on the surface, but just underneath.
So when it surfaces,
The receiver is caught off guard,
Shocked and made numb, struck dumb
By the vicious and compelling attack,
The giver aware subconsciously, but under
The illusion that everything is okay…
In fact, nothing is okay until the pain is
Faced, dealt with, brought to the surface
And stilled.
I am thoroughly convinced,
That only God can still it, bring it to the surface,
And snuff what lies beneath.

I Choose to Forgive…

…even when the anger is prevalent.
…even when the hurt and offense
is fresh in mind and heart.

…even when the offender is unrepentant
and excuse-driven.

…even when there is no rhyme or reason
behind the actions.

…even when the offense is forgotten, and sleep seems
to be sweet
for the one who caused the wound
While sleep evades the wounded.

…even when the pain of the offender
is so deeply rooted, it is unseen to the
one who forgiveness is required of.

…even when the problems exist deep within the perpetrator
and
without a cause, lashes out and doesn't even know why,
bitter beyond comprehension,
heart filled with tangled knots
of animosity, strife, envy, resentment
and every evil thing wrapped up all in it,
still unknown and suppressed by the victim,
who has become the victimizer,
The oppressed, who has become the oppressor,

The offended, who has become the great offender,
The one in need of deliverance…

...even then.

...with strength given from above to do so.
...to love freely and continue in that love.
...to accept deliverance and remain delivered.
...to *be* free and *stay* free.

...to be forgiven.

Inspiration

Chapter 2

THE SKY IS MY FLOOR
An Ode to Divine Inspiration

I am limitless!
Unfathomably rich in love, in life, in wealth, in health,
in *Christ Jesus*.
Able to walk on clouds that are jumping pads into space!
I walk and trot through worlds' trails,
Blazing my mark across the expansive star gate…

My gaze surpasses constellations and galaxies – next stop:
Heaven!
I spend quality time with my Father God, *Most High* and
mingle with the angels.
My dining arrangements are on the sun,
The moon, my canopy, when I settle down to relax.
The Milky Way is my vacation spot –
The stars, my choice of travel.

I anticipate the day with wonder, joy unfathomable,
A peace much unlike anything you could ever explain.
It's what I do: travel, build, think anew, love, live
…and *fly*.

The sky is my floor,
And I am limitless!

When I Look Forward to the Backfire
Inspired by Psalm 7

When I dig a ditch of good for someone else and fall into it myself.
When I conceive kindness, am pregnant with empathy, and have a compassion baby.
When I plot plans to aid people, and they all come back on me.
When I devise strategies of peace against others, and it all comes crashing down on me.
When I go around gossiping about all the great things happening to people, and it comes back around.
When I spread all these truths about folk, and all of them breed honesty.
When I build weapons of mass benevolence, and all of them are used on me.
When I spew words of life, growing everything in my path, and they all come back to haunt me.
When I do all that I can to make others' lives a living heaven, and I get all the heaven that's due me.

LIGHT IT UP!

When you feel the fire from your pen
Start to burn your hand,

Light it up!

When you want that fire to leap out onto
The paper and singe the heart,

Light it up!

When you feel the words smoldering in your mind
Ready to burst forth like an inferno,

Light it up!

Even when you feel no one else is feeling your fire,
Burning up with imparted knowledge and gifted word,

Light it up!

When the dissin'
Criticisms, skepticism
And all other isms,
Cross your heated communiqué,

Light it up!

When it seems, the hearts are not touched by the licks
Of your internal flame,

When all is silent, and you hear
No passionate,

No dispassionate
Replies, while you're letting your sparks fly
Across a global page,

Light It Up!

For when the world finally feels your fire and you
Blow up before your eyes and theirs,
It will not consume you because
You were burning all along.

Dedications

Chapter 3

HER GRADUATION
To C.R.P.

Stepping the stone,
Dreaming a little dream,
Coming to a place,
In your life of meaning...

Divine Queen,
Daughter of God,
Sister of Jesus Christ,
La Negra,
Woman Graduate,
Clytheia.

And here she stands, head held high,
Graceful poise, steadfast gaze,
Ready to face her world to come.
A stride of confidence,
Purpose, determination, peace,
Rest in God.

So I've been told, to believe in flight.
Yet, you may say: 'I have flown.'
And here you are soaring, in flight,
Gliding across the stage.

Eyes follow you on your way,
Those of pride, joy, happiness, sharing
Your moment, your time, with you.
A symbol of triumph, of achievement,
A time past, she receives with gladness,
In her heart, mind, and *spirit*.

The celebration has begun and the embrace
Of they who celebrate with her.
Her soul and her intellect are touched by an *angel*,
And she is ready to move higher and higher,
For she has been there before.

HERE YOU ARE AT 30
To H.B.C.

It seems like your world is turned upside down,
But it's being turned right side up.
It seems like your life is leading to an end,
But it's just beginning.

It seems like your life is topsy-turvy,
But here is where it starts to get balanced.
It seems like your life is getting old,
But it's brand spankin' new.

Here you are at 30.

And this is where you say:
"I don't give a ____ [fill in accordingly]
If you like me or not.
I love me for me.

You need to love me for me.
And if you don't,
Well, that's alright with me.
I still love you
And I still love me."

A time of acceptance for who you are,
And what you bring to the table,
Not enabling others by worrying about,
What they want you to bring.

A time of assessing your strengths
And your weaknesses,
Building from each,
Looking at what you can do,
What God can do…
And nothing more.

A time not to over think,
But think for yourself.
A time for being concerned about others,
And not what they think.

God has blessed you with life
And another opportunity,
To show you and the world who you are,
And not what they want you to be.

A blessing to yourself,
Those around you and those to come,
Being there for others,
While fellowshipping with others,
Who are there for you.

Confidently aware of your exterior and interior beauty
You, and others who know you, can see.
You accept you, and they accept you,
For each and every quality that is yours.

Be excited for this time,
Sublime, in line, Sister girl,
With what God has created
You and yours to be and become.

Let Jesus continue to love and fill you
Through and through,
Knowing you are complete in Him,
Though He's not through completing you.

With hands to the hips and head held high, say:
"Hello, world! My name is *Haniyyah*, and

Here I am at 30!"

AND SO THERE IS DOROTHY MAE
To D.M.Y. – Matriarch

And God looked down from heaven.
The world seemed incomplete.
There was something missing…
"I will make me a daughter that makes life sweet and full of adventure."
Her life was born, formed by her Elohim.
Designed, created and shaped with purpose, fearfully and wonderfully made.
And so there was Dorothy Mae Flourise Lavenia…

And God saw that she was good. She was complete. In Him.
Mocha and Lovely,
A Queen in her own right –
Queen of Sheba and Madea all in one.
Sugar and Spice and all that is nicety –
Sweet chocolate with a bite,
A tender lamb seasoned with hot sauce.

And so there was Dorothy Mae…
A rose by any other name is just not as sweet,
Hailing from a strong lineage and caring guidance,
She carries a legacy filled with the Blessing of the Lord, wisdom and strength.
Having birthed her own generation,
Her legacy remains, with Jesus all wrapped up in it.
Her offspring, five pillars who carry on her heritage,
Pass them down to those who inherit her legacy for many generations to come.
Called Mother by many hues and nations,
Sarah, of the Good Book, may have met her match.

A strong, classy, womanly matriarch and wife,
Enjoying her golden years with her husband and partner in love and peace,
She is maxing and relaxing in her golden age.

And so there is Dorothy Mae…
She is loved, cherished, and revered, definitively and positively impacting the lives
Of Family, friends, and strangers alike.
Having made and continuing to make an indelible, impressionable, and memorable
Mark, deeply touching the lives of those she encounters.
Now we see her, and she has made it through many an adversity, continuing to
Rise through the trials with tremendous victory, she wins and has won in Jesus' name.

And so there is Dorothy Mae…
She has been given several titles throughout her life's journey: Dotsy, Sugarboy, Dot, The Black Orchid, Mrs. Young, Mother, Ma, Grammy, *Gram Gram*.
Many seasons have passed,
Many summers…many springs…
Many winters…many falls…
Many mornings and many nights…
Time has passed…and she stands strong.

And so here is Dorothy Mae…
And God sees that she is good. She is complete. In Him.

HE KNEW HOW TO BE A FATHER
To H.W.Y. – Patriarch

God gave him a family.
He came and took care of that family,
A family not his own...

Because he knew how to be a father.

"I'll help you raise your family, your children,
I will make you, them, my own."

He became *Daddy*,
Not the sugar kind, but the sweet kind,
Who offered love with no strings.
He became a father,
To a family he needed and loved,
As if he birthed them in his loins himself.

A loving father, husband, he became over the years,
Without a care for himself,
Stealthily, caringly, compassionately,
Patiently, lovingly,
He entered the hearts and minds
Of generation after generation:
Daughters and sons,
Granddaughters and grandsons,
Great granddaughters and great grandsons.

Biological semantics did not count,
Blood ties were formed through
Spiritual, soulish, and psychological ties,
Melting away the trivial.

He knew how to be a father.

It came naturally to call him *Daddy*.
No matter how the story began,
It became of the story of a father
Who found his family...
Whose family found him.
"My wife and my children."
"My husband / our Daddy."

He loved, and he comforted,
Cajoled and spoiled them.
He laughed, and he cried with them,
He disciplined, and he corrected them,
He taught them wisdom and knowledge,
How to dance, to fish,
To be what they want to be, to love.

And his descendants will remember,
Note for many generations to come,
His namesake, his legacy,
His love, his compassion, his laugh, his selflessness,
That continues through them.

God gave him a family.
He took care of that family,
A family now his own...

Because he knew how to be a Father.

JOSEPH DOES RISE
To Pastor E.A.B. (Inspired by Genesis 39)

Though vacant is the box,
Where the cheers come from the fickle crowd.
Though the choice of many may not be for him who
Clings to the vision he was called to bring forth,
He has the Wonderful Counselor in his corner.

There are those who plan and plot,
Eyes covered with dust and soot,
Masquerading in Jesus' name.
Lips lifted high in praise, not to reach heaven –
Their hearts in the gutter.

One vote, one gamble,
The brothers throw him into the pit…
The dead bones stand around the edge,
Unknowingly assisting the vision,
That will surely come to pass.

They seek to throw the boy away,
To steal, kill, and destroy,
The coat of blood,
A visible manifestation of their wicked reality,
As they encounter the spiritual reality
Of the man he will become.

Sickness,
Pain,
Time and labor,
He toils both day and night –
Yet, he is free.

The spirit of Potiphar's wife consumes them,
And lust appears to reign,
Yet the place of addition
Is hidden in the cell he occupies.

In the spirit, the plan has been set:
One man. One vision. One ministry.
Sent to touch the hardened hearts
Of the *heart* of the Commonwealth.

He stands in Jesus' name,
Imparting pure knowledge
To the listening ears of those who
Have joined the vision and with him,
Have become one.

The rejected cornerstone has found
Its place in the Kingdom.
He has become only Second-in-Command
To the King of kings and the Lord of lords.

In a land of spiritual famine,
Here, where they hunger and thirst:
Before him, they will bow…

And just as God's story has shown once before:

Joseph does rise.

SITUATIONAL CANCER
To the Innocent

Blackface.
Frankenstein's monster rearing its ugly head
In the guise of "good, clean fun".
Asking "What did we do?"
While demonstrating inhuman qualities
By spurning the pain and tragedy of the targeted parody.
No shame. No compassion. No heart.
Just spreading and parasitically remaining attached to the host
Of deep seated hatred, jealousy, insecurity, and fear:
"What I did to you, will you do to me?"
Spreading and spreading from generation to generation
Killing the host, the perpetrator, more than the target.
A painful debacle, yet keeps spreading because the ones
Spreading it have a tendency toward violence and hate
And can't seem to let it go.
Hiding behind religion that has nothing to do with Jesus.
Calling his name and saying *Hallelujah* doesn't
Take away your human stain,
Your stench is palpable and horrid,
Spewing toxic waste as you vilify and cheer the murder
Of an innocent Black…Young…Elder…Man. Woman.
…Child.
Their blood continues to speak as Abel's.
Go ahead and tie the proverbial neck ornament –
That millstone and go jump in the nearest body of water,
You and your encouragers,
Because that is your best fate.
You don't see it comin',

But you will pay for your sins: hard, cold, brutal, and fast.
Don't think you won't pay because it comes down to this:
The truth will make you free.
And we will all get to see the vindication
Of the innocent blood
That was shed…
When the cancer is cut out –
And the parasite dies thrashing and alone.

Tired (Bully)

Tired of the bullying.
Tired of the confronting.
Tired of the confrontations…

Tired of the frontin'.
Tired of the sense of entitlement.
Tired of the audacity
That comes with bullying
Someone into doing what you want.

Tired of the chaos,
The *say whats*?
The can't believes
Because I wouldn't do,

Tired of it happening to me
Because I look younger than I do.

Tired of the confrontations
That bring about offense
And uncomfortable feelings,
The resentment,
Displacement, and playback recordings
Of incidents: "I should have",
"I would have", "I could have".
Tired of the regrets, feeling small
With intimidation, undermined
By another because of their selfish
Intimations.

I can't help it if you want something I have.
I can't help it if you want what's not yours.
I can't help it if you try to intimidate me.
But I can help you *stop* it with me.

Tired of the bullying.
Tired of the confronting.
Tired of the confrontations…

I will make it stop
With a sound reaction…
And the bullying will cease.

PLANTED BY THE RIVER * (Call and Response)
To the Joshua Generation

Planted by the river,
Nestled in the topsoil are the remains...
"Can these bones live?"
"Yes." Whispered on the wind.

The Word breathes Life in them,
They begin to rise,
One by one connecting as Life's breath
Strengthens their surging bones...
"Can these bones move?"
"Yes." Whispered on the wind.

With sinew and marrow and flesh rushing to them,
Attaching to the skeletal frames as if coming home,
Their frames heave with weary sighs
That transform into sighs of relief – of release...
"Can these bones have their being?"
"Yes." Whispered on the wind.

The massive force strengthened by Life's breath,
Moves with precision and in one accord,
To the rushing waters –
They dip and drink thirstily in syncopation,
Soothing their palates and vocal chords...

Quenched thirst,
Manifold miniature waves rippling through
Muscular, respiratory, endocrine, nervous,

Soulish and spiritual systems...
Coursing through arteries, veins, nerves,

Commingling with the fluid of Life,
Satiating their heart, mind, intellect, and spirit.

They rise fully soaked,
They heave with a contented sigh,
As their thirst is quenched…

They stand with faces turned heavenward,
With eyes shuttered, while eyelashes and eyelids drink.
They listen to hear the Word…
They hear: "Welcome, Joshua!"
Whispered on the wind.

Arms outstretched in the shape of a V,
Liquid pouring through their hands, their fingers,
Seeping through the lines of their palms,
Lining the veins raised under their newborn skin…
They cry out in one accord a loud cry of total praise:
"Hallelujah!"
Carried on the wind.

Together as one,
Their facial muscles are extended portraying
A visage of pure joy and unmerited peace,
Understanding unmerited grace…unmerited favor.
They remain planted by the river of living water,

The army waiting for their marching orders,
Steeped in the Holy Ghost's measure of Faith,
Equally given, equally measured, equally potent:

They receive the Faith of El Elyon – Elohim – El Shaddai!
God Most High – God with us – God Almighty!
The remnant, born and raised up in Jesus as Joshua,

As Glory wraps them,
They stand hardened to fight the good fight of faith:
They stand strong.
They stand *ready*.

       * Ezekiel 37 (King James Version)

MS. PERFECTION SAYS GOODBYE
To We Girls and Women

Looking in the mirror,
I bid farewell.
She stares back in amazement,
Because I have let her go.
No more do I believe the lies
Pouring from her lips.

She rants at me with a twisted grin:
YOU ARE too ugly.
YOU ARE too fat.
YOU ARE weak.
YOU ARE not good enough.
YOU ARE stupid and
YOU ARE dumb.
YOU ARE incapable of doing anything.

I cry louder:
I AM Impeccably made!
I AM All that is Beautiful!
I AM Strong!
I AM Intelligent!
And I will say again:
I AM *very* Intelligent!
I AM capable of doing Everything!

I close my eyes and breathe:
I AM ME.

No longer can she demand from me the impossible:
To be other than myself.

Through
All *my* perfection,
All *my* imperfection,
All *my* passion,
All *my* pain,
All *my* joy,
All *my* sorrow,
All *my* good,
Annnnnnd
All *my* ugly:
I AM AND WILL ALWAYS BE ME.

I open my eyes.

She glares at me,
Angry,
Aware, her control has slipped away.

I smile in return,
Elated,
Aware, I am free.

Laughter explodes from my lips,
And a tear from my eye,
As I watch her fade…

Knowing,
At that spectacular and long-awaited moment,
I will no longer look in the mirror…
And cry.

Scriptures

Chapter 4

SNOWFLAKE *

The snowflake:
A crystallized pattern,
Made up of a unique nature –
Not one ever the same.

As peculiar as a singular fingerprint,
No replica or imitation is ever
Like the original – untouched in beauty.

Mirror like semblances do not mask
What is of its own kind – its DNA,
Unexplainable and unfathomable
To the heart of man, yet not to God,
Who created the same.

We are as the snowflake.
There is no one like no one else.
Hard as we might try to be otherwise,
When we are ourselves, it becomes easy
To see clearly…no longer blinded
By an image of someone else's beauty,
Not seeing our own.

We are able to see within ourselves
The *deep calling to the deep*,
Facets unlike anyone else.
An appreciation of the weaknesses,

Buoying the strengths within –
Together creating a distinctive combination.
Acceptance and joy and peace and love,
Because understanding and revelation

Has enlightened our spiritual reality,
Enabling us to see who God says we are.

Unlike anything or anyone else:
We see our crystallized pattern,
Made up of a unique nature –
Not one ever the same.

                          * Psalm 42:7 (King James Version)

EVER PRESENT *

Crazy as it may seem,
Life has not treated me so mean.
With my Maker as my Protector…
Why should I complain?

Life seems to throw me jabs,
Air rushes from my lungs through stabs,
And shortness of breath is common perhaps…
Yet, I'm breathing.

My habit of tears staining my clothes,
My lying down with eyes closed,
Wondering if I could ever break the mold,
And when I look down, I see a small, broken piece,
The size of a hand's palm I suppose…
Still, I feel the release.

Days of wondering what did I do?
To deserve the pain of missteps and wounds,
Disappointments and hurts and freshly scarred anew
Tissue marred from painful decisions…
Withal, the blood clots and the scabs begin to form.

With knowledge filled eyes,
I've come to realize,
That in the midst of pain,
Healing is powerfully present…
All the time.

        * 1 Kings 18:41-46 (v44) (King James Version)

TALENT *

I don't want Jesus
To find my talent
In the dirt.

I don't want to hide it,
Bury it,
Deep in the dirt.

He planted it in me,
To grow.
It's there,
The talents – double the weight.

When He comes back,
I want Him to have
The ten He's looking for.

* Matthew 25:20 (King James Version)

ACT *

What Word have I heard so strongly in my ear?
The claim of belief has permeated my soul.
The sinews of my flesh have spoken,
In a whisper. In the dark.
I hear myself speak in the recesses of my mind:
I repeat: He heals.
I sing: He loves.
I proclaim: He cannot lie.

A cloud has clouded my vision.
One small, ambiguous image,
There and I see it.
It has become rain.
It has become a tornado,
Whipping me to and fro,
"And having done all to stand,
Stand therefore…"

It has come to the forefront of my mind.
The Word that has breached my spirit,
Has not been reached in the natural.
My application fails.

It is time to use what has been given me.
The gift of spoken word requires
Faith as the engine, the locomotive
With which I have to move.

Emotional whirlwind.
I must step out beyond the pinnacles of doubt and

Stand on the word that was told
By the Man who heals, loves, and cannot lie.
My only risk:
To *act*.

                    * Ephesians 6:13-14 (King James Version)

My Relationship with God

Chapter 5

God is (...) Good

(oh soooo)
(well-shaped afro)
(soul food)
(great conversation)
(sun on my face)
(dancing with myself)
(watchin' a movie the zillionth time
as if it's the first time)
(running through a fire hydrant fountain)
(gospel music jam)
(warm smile)
(old soul)
(laughing 'til you can't stop)
(husband and wife sweet vibes)
(enjoying being with family)
(friend being a friend)
(joy after the pain)
(heaven on earth)
(answer to all your problems)
(awesomely)
(intoxicatingly)
(is just what He is)

WHAT IT'S LIKE

Spending time with God is like...

...seeing lilies that are full grown
demonstrating all their glory...

...watching the sparrow
that never goes hungry...

...*hakuna matata* when it comes to what to wear,
eat, drink, and pay bills...

...chewing on a *really* tender piece of seasoned steak
while savoring the taste...

...walking with purposeful strides to a desired
destination and making it there *on time*...

...walking through a sea of grass
with the dew on your feet in the *warm-cool* of the day...

...watching the sunrise in all its splendor
in a peaceful place...

...sitting on the boardwalk with two scoops of
chocolate-vanilla swirl soft serve melting in your mouth...

...breathing a contented sigh while sitting in a quiet
park surrounded by trees, the scent of flowers, and a slight
breeze on your skin...

...listening to a right on time tune while chilling
in your place of comfort...

...lounging on a hammock drinking a cool drink
on a warm summer day...

...relaxing in front of a crackling fire sipping a cup of hot cocoa
on a cold winter day...

...talking to a good friend who understands
what you're talking about at the time you're talking about it...

...being in a relationship that has Him as the center, encompasses
love and prayer and fosters coming and reasoning together...

...having someone who is attentive to your every detail
and you attentive to theirs...

...sweet fellowship that is continuous and a relationship
that is rewarding to each other...

...having peace when it seems that there
is none to be had...

...loving and having love when love is not present
around you...

...forgiving and obtaining forgiveness when
it is not deserving or deserved...

...*seeing* impossibilities, but *knowing*
they are possibilities because of Him...

...knowing that His and your purposeful words fulfill what
they are sent to accomplish irrelevant of the circumstance...

...knowing that praise encourages, propels hope, and empowers
with faith when reason to hope and believe is gone...

...hearing and experiencing the awesome power
held in the name of Jesus and *knowing* it's real...

...feeling so good at the moment you realize
that all is right with your world, even if seems it isn't
because He is all up in it.

That is what it's like.

Dust *

God remembers...
That we are nothin' but dust
Without Him.

An empty shell, well formulated
Walking around on death row,
Wondering how we were
Fearfully and wonderfully made.

Rejecting the notion that the shell
Had to be created by *Somebody*,
Yet still have no clue about
How the shell was formed.
So, we're useless...nothin' but dust.

Being clay dwellers and all,
Just seems so empty and *dusty*,
Without Him.

I dare say, my speaking spirit,
Fills this empty shell when I
Speak with Him and find out
What makes me tick either way.

Who am I and why am I on earth?
I'm here with the notion,
That I was made on purpose.

I'm more than an eating, toiling machine,
Made up of nothin' but dust.

Come to find out, I *was* made on purpose.
So, I am more than a working, food filler.
It is *such* a pleasure to finally know,
My dust wiping days are not in vain.

Jesus has been with me always…
And I can't live without Him.

     * Genesis 2:7 (King James Version)

TEARS IN YOUR BOTTLE *

Tears in Your bottle…
Do not escape.
They are captured in Your eternal embrace.

Cuddled and coddled, free to feel peace,
Strengthened and guarded by Your sweet release.

No longer to feel shame or guilt, terror, or fear,
Released from the pain of many past years,

Sorrow replaced by joy,
With no anguish in between,
But rather a peace and serenity,
That cannot be explained.

Tears in your bottle…
No, they will never escape,
Embraced by Your love,
Quenched from heartache.

Happy with joy,
Drenched and no shame,
I thank God – You placed

My tears in Your bottle…

And gave me Jesus instead.

> * Psalm 56:8 (King James Version)

Everything is about Color

Chapter 6

Color Carries Feeling

Color carries feeling,
Some mistakenly so by a misrepresentation of pigment, or the lack thereof,
As deified by western culture
By any other phrase, is just not that sweet...
But for *real* though...

Color carries feeling,
Sometimes I look at red on the keyboard and that red just gets on my nerve,
But a moment ago, maybe more, I was *feeling* that red.
Don't know why, one of those things that fall under the weirdly unexplainable.
Ok, so what was I saying?

Color carries feeling,
Albeit some feelings are false, led by a westernized culture that demonizes based on
How much color is present:
Good color...when you don't have it...like that makes sense.
Bad color...when you have a lot of it...like that makes any more sense.
I heard black was beautiful and classic and *cocktail dressy*.
Then, I heard black was ugly and weird and utterly strange.

This is all so confusing.
I heard white was pale and ghastly and leprous.
Then, I heard white was pure and milky and *creamy*.
This is all so *very* confusing.
But for *real* though...

Color carries feeling,
Blue always makes me feel good…but sky blue gives me peace…royal blue, makes me feel
Well…royal, and then there's neon blue…I'll have to rethink that one.
Ok, as I was saying…

Color carries feeling,
I feel it every day…when I sit in front of my computer, when I walk through a seedy, racist
Neighborhood, when I encounter a white supremacist couched in friendly conversation…*oops!*
The cat's out of the bag.
But for *real* though…

Color does carry feeling,
Pink is an interesting shade, not so much, unless it's lavender…I really *like* lavender.

Mocha Chocolate-Skinned

Mocha-Chocolate Skinned.
Butter-Toffee Skinned.
Coffee Skinned.
Orange-Blossom Skinned.
Ebony Skinned.
Coffee-with-Cream Skinned.
Onyx Skinned.
Butterscotch Skinned.
Milk Chocolate Skinned.
Praline Skinned.

God's Choice Skinned.

There is no dark skinned.
There is no light skinned.

Just color. Just hue. Just human.

Vestiges of slavery linger...
Heavy. Tragic.
Disparaging. Negative.
Divisive. Deceptive.
Angry. Contentious.
Hurtful. Disdainful.
False. Unjust.
Created. Illusion.
Delusion. Projected.
Protected. Legated.
By them. By us.
Shame on them. Shame on us.

I let go.
You let go.
We let go.

My skin: Beautiful.
Your skin: Beautiful.
Our skin: Beautiful.

Umber Skinned.
Mauve Skinned.
Black Diamond Skinned.
Beach-Sand Skinned.
Sapphire Skinned.
Sun-Rain Skinned.
Cedar-in-Lebanon Skinned.
Amaretto Skinned.
Almond Skinned.
Peanut Butter Skinned.

God's Choice Skinned.

There is no dark skinned.
There is no light skinned.

Just color. Just hue. Just human.

Observations, Reminiscences, Reflections

Chapter 7

These are Kind of Like Thoughts

These are kind of like thoughts:

Poetry.

The unspeakable speaks,
Life gifted without flatlining,
And paper is all in all,
To the contemplations-as-words revealed.

If it remains behind the eyes only, *well then*.

It would be thoughts —
This sort-of-poetry…
Speaking the unspeakable,
Only keeping it to yourself.

PRISONER

To be a *prisoner of hope*:

Depending on the goodness of God,
Looking at a desperate situation and seeing
That at any moment it can change,

Seeing pain while knowing healing,
Fully comprehending that the burden you carry
Is lighter and the yoke is easier,
Leaning on His abiding strength
In your weakest times,

Learning from the Good Book,
That Jesus is my Truth,
And my Salvation and my Peace,
And my Food and my Supply.

Knowing that I am not alone,
That I am deeply loved with an everlasting love,
That no matter the situation,
In Jesus Christ, I will triumph,
Leading me to find that even in chains,
I am free.

From this prison I wish to never escape.

SHE LOVED ME MORE

She stopped. I stopped.
She looked at me. I looked back.
She opened her mouth to speak. I listened.
Encourage yourself. Why bother with anything else?
Don't be discouraged or led by what others think –
Do you really know anyway?
Reading minds has never been anyone's strong suit.
If someone shows you their limitations by their artificial interpretations,
What does that have to do with you?
You were fearfully and wonderfully made.
And you are flawed. Get over it!
Don't hold it against yourself. God doesn't.
He made you. So become you.
You have a bio suit of armor that covers another suit of armor: your spirit.
Get to know your spirit. Get to know you.
Others will try to crowd you with their own projections. Their own flaws.
Their own faults. Their own hurt. Their own misery.
You don't have to take it. You don't have to receive it.
Receive encouragement. Receive yourself.
She fell silent. Silent, I remained.
She smiled. I smiled.
The smile translated through her spirit.
It roiled into her soul.
It connected to her flesh.
And slid into her eyes.
She stayed silent. I looked away from the mirror.

T-I-S Tizzz

Practically searching for that reward,
That feeling of soaring affection,
Happiness or joy onset by clear circumstances,
Life, whispering words of callous behavior that take
Away the clarity,
Leaving me wondering, yet understanding…
That's just how it T-I-S tizzz.

Walking along an embankment,
Given over to such as it is and
I hear the melancholy blows
Of the saxophonist, his words,
Calling through the sound of his mellifluous horn,
He sends a message of pleasure and pain,
Leaving me wondering, yet understanding…
That's just how it T-I-S tizzz.

Falling into the heavenly abyss,
That without a floor,
No stopping,
Just suspended in mid-air,
Feeling that exhilarating and excruciating
Living called love,
Leaving me wondering, yet understanding…
That's just how it T-I-S tizzz.

AUSTIN

Chicago's best kept secret:
Right between the narrow-minded and the blinded.

Though the city plays favorites through the CTA train lines,
Two lines takes us to the land of milk and honey.
The Green Line takes us to green pastures,
The Blue Line to Royalty, kings and queens in their own right.

Community pillars and fighters, fighting the good fight of faith,
Austin's finest – the residents – parade through with confidence.
Knowing they are the diamond in the mines,
Hewn from the best coal, hidden in onyx,
The best kind is the raw kind,
The west side is the best side:
So start mining.

Little gold nuggets hidden in plain sight –
Little Davids telling the Goliaths to back up!

Don't look to the North or to the South, or to the East –
Look to the West side: Chicago's *best kept secret*.

Chest Pain

There's a time in your life when hard times reign,
But keep your head up, so you won't go insane...
Don't refrain from yelling out loud,
When you feel like bursting, for crying out loud!

Let it go when it's time to do,
Don't let the pain ensue...
The void can't be filled with more and more pain,
That will only lead you back to blame upon blame,
Guilt, fear, resentment, and a constant chest pain...
That can't be erased by *antacids*.

What if I tell you that your deliverance can come?
Through what I call the talking drum...
The communication level that reaches past due,
That can alleviate some of the stress on the chest and lift you,
A little higher, a little higher, and a little higher some more.

What of it when you give it some thought, some tries, and some seeking,
The answer may be in the wings of your mouth when it starts talking...
Lettin' your voice be heard through the words that fall from your mouth,
When you call to your Source: *The Most High*!

Let the sore spots be healed and the wounds cleaned out!
That's part of the hard part...in that I have no doubt.
Life doesn't get easier with or without the bling...
But it sure feels so much better without the chest pain.

OPPORTUNITY

Take it while you can.
Don't wait to bless the next man or woman or child.

Seize it while it's near
Held dear by the one you bless,
And by the One who blesses...

The Father, who sees in secret,
Tells the secret with an open reward,
In hand, brought back to you by His
Grace, mercy, and Omniscience...

God is a God of *payback*,
Gives blessing because of your need,
Met by the seed planted,
In the life of the man or woman or child
You blessed.

I seized it while it was near
Held dear by the one I blessed
And the One who blesses...

And the Father who saw it in secret,
Brazenly *told all*,
With my open reward.

GIVE

It's coming back to me:
What I give, what I do.

What will be my reciprocal?
Good treasure?
Not so much?

Wishful thinking…naw.
Faith is all I'm believing for —
What I receive.

I'm aiming for the Good Treasure.

I'll know when it gets here.
Not by *how* much —
It's always gonna be *too* much.

But I'll know by the comeback…
It will always be about the comeback.

WHERE I GREW (A Narrative Poem)

I grew up in this place coined *the Valley*.

A project built for Silent Gen veterans,

But then Silent Gen, Baby Boom, and Gen X Black folk moved there.

Near Wotown's outskirts –

Actually known as *Wormtown* – aka *Wootown* – aka *Wotown* –

Not sure of the evolution of monikers,

But *I say*, probably because being called a worm ain't so cool,

And hey, the other names sound cooler – *esque*.

So, I'll say *Wotown*.

When the veterans lived there, it was looked upon well.

But then, was re-branded a *project* –

When Black folk moved in,

At times, *predominantly*. (Clears throat).

All of a sudden, life became *rough. Asterisk.*

With cultures, at times, *non-predominantly / predominantly* sprinkled in between,

We lived.

I guess it was rough, you know, growing up in the Valley,

With my door unlocked,

And neighbors looking out for my home.

Walking through the neighborhood with my girlfriends,

We gave everyone one, young and old, a holla.

I gather this response was never far from the lips:

"Tell Mr. and Mrs. So and So…Tell your grandmother and grandfather…Tell your mother…Tell your sisters, Tell your family: *How you doing?*

Those black folks, with their neighborly ways, would sit and watch and listen and greet us, as if they knew us so well.

You could say, I learned that having black friends was not a trying-to-convince-me-I'm-not-a racist card play,

But me being black and all, with my whole being, I knew and understood, and found firsthand,

Having black friends was a blessing.

It was rough,

Seeing my first home garden next to the townhouse I grew up in with my family, and the screen doors painted different colors according to the family's wishes,

Mine, baby blue –

Before the housing authority made all the doors uniform colors, took our screen doors, and barred up the windows like military barracks.

You know, it was *trying* when we played those baseball games with a plastic bat and whiffle ball in the back of the house, playing all over the grassy knolls that were sprinkled heavily throughout the neighborhood,

Where we played and ran and giggled whether we were chased – or not;

Searching for those Easter eggs during the egg hunts, plastic eggs of pink, yellow, and white all behind the trees and backs of buildings, just waiting for the family to grab 'em;

Making snow angels in all of that snow, and Auntie making hot chocolate for us kids after we purposely made our faces cold;

And playing with Mr. and Ms. So and So's little daughters and little sons in the heaping backyard-on-a hill that covered the span of our connected townhouses.

There were those local kids who didn't steal our Halloween candy because they knew our family name.

And then there was this seventh sense, when we knew who was the new-to-the-neighborhood kid, formed our own welcoming committee, and went to greet with a question of utmost importance: *Do you want to come out and play?*

Let me not forget the summertime, when I watched the fine young wiry guys, black skin glistening, walking up and down the street, wearing muscle tees, moving to a blaring rhythm, with stereos bigger than them, resting high on their shoulders.

Then there was the neighbor's grown son we always greeted with excitement, because he looked like the Black Jesus on the lithograph in my living room with his chocolate skin and curly curls.

And then there was Ms. So and So, and the neighbor's daughter who would braid my hair in those cool styles so I could walk around looking fresh, with my hair *done*.

There were those times when we'd be picked up and dropped off to the legendary Aunt Essie's daycare – from preschool to Kindergarten – by Mr. So and So from the neighborhood, while Mom worked.

Sometimes we'd stay with Mrs. So and So, until we were picked up, and it was somewhat cool to hang out, until 3:00 pm when *her story* came on – the one I liked was on a different channel –

Where we'd buy fried chicken dinners from Mrs. So and So, with yellow potato salad, collard greens, rice, and hot water cornbread – even though I preferred the Jiffy cornbread because it was sweeter.

I cannot help but mention where I learned *yes ma'am* and *yes sir*, politely speaking, and *don't talk to strangers*, and where later, someone had to tell me I was poor, because I didn't feel it…and saying to me I was poor didn't change that…

And where the entrepreneurial fish lady and egg roll lady came through the neighborhood.

Then there was the extended invitation, year after year to a party, celebrating the life of a little girl called Lucy, where I learned to like rice and beans and to hate flan.

All those things…*I don't know how I made it through.*

Running to the store around the corner and the lady selling candy inside her house, and saying *hey* to the kids hanging out, before and after buying banana squirrels.

Right in the grassy center, at this, you know, community festival, I learned how to ride a pony for the first time, and it got easier and easier every year I could remember.

That could be a bit scary…until it wasn't.

Going to a neighbor's house to buy limbers, and then becoming an entrepreneur alongside my sisters, to sell our own limbers for a quarter, and lemonade for a dime –

That was crazy.

Then there was this brother who would lend me his basketball at 7:00 in the morning, and there was this Puerto Rican boy who taught me how to do a layup in the neighborhood courtyard,

Where'd I'd sit and yearn over my first crushes battling out with sweat, laughter, trash talkin' and friendship building over a basketball and a net –

The too-old-for me tall, lanky mocha-skinned boy was my longest crush.

I guess you could say seeing a whole community of pre-teen and teen boys, you know, surround our car, and push our dead SUV up the hill so

We could get the car to "jump" in the dead of winter, while I was in it…

That was wild.

I don't know if I could abide the craziness of all of those *Valley* people, who, no matter the cultural countenance, would see my Grammy walking through the neighborhood,

And say or *scream* with all their might if they felt she was too far away to hear them: *Hey Mother!*

I guess you could say it was tough, when this Puerto Rican neighbor, cradled my mother in his arms and brought her to the door, after she, exhausted, fell asleep in her car, gas running; he gathered her belongings,

And with nothing missing, nothing broken, brought her to my grandmother's house.

There it was, this place I was accused of knowing nothing of, my own stomping ground, because, you know, I guess I wasn't considered rough enough to live up to its notorious-like legend.

So let's see…you got your love, community, love for learning new things, love for family, love for friends, learning to start new businesses, friend-like family and family-like friends, compassion, people who care, caring people, and people caring, and all the details that make you love who you are…

Funny, how I learned, while living there – *where it was rough* – how to embrace those things.

Funny, I guess…how I learned this wonderful litany above, in the rough *sweetness*,
With Black folk.

Wait a minute –

I did learn bad words in Spanish so...

This is where I grew up, in the Valley.

This is where I *grew*.

Asterisk: rough: to be clear, meaning depicted as *rough* because of Black demographics, though the community environment was *family-oriented* and *built character*...you know...just in case someone needed further explanation. (Clears throat). Thank you.

Breakthrough

Tides are calling…
I walk in them,
And break up the tides.

I don't know why I am here.

Maybe it's a trial.
Maybe it's the journey.

But I know one thing…

I've broken through.
I've broken through.

Men Don't Leave

"Daddy, where are you going?"
"I'm just going out the door, honey
I'll be back..."
Eyes filled with tears,
She watches as he closes the door.

He's left before,
When she was a toddler, now ten.
Again, he shows up at the same door.

Mama's feet are tired from working long hours.
At dawn, she leaves the house,
Not to return 'til twilight.
Sister cooks the dinner –
Sister, still a child.

Now he walks through the door,
With a smile and a pick-me-up,
As if his feet didn't tread elsewhere for seven years.
Soda, a bag of chips, and a movie, a few dollars.

I guess that makes up for the time
Mama took on the role of daddy,
The years sister became second mother.

No parents at the school play,
Awards night.
One haggard smile for the 'A's on the report card,
A weary embrace to comfort tears shed.

Yet now we get to hear the hollow promises,
A few *dulces* to sugarcoat the years of anguish,
Good times created in the bad.

Mama doing what she can to make ends out of one dollar.
Many numbers:
One paycheck, 60 hours, three children.
Knowing the voice of bill collectors
More than daddy's voice.
So here he goes, out the door.

And little brother watches with big eyes,
Soaring on the empty promise,
"I'll be back…"

As sister walks across the stage
And accepts her Baccalaureate of Science,
Mama sits in the crowd with me and little brother,
Lit up with smiles of pride, joy, resignation –
The seat empty next to him.

Sundry Times

...we eat.
...we drink.
...we wake.
...we sleep.
...we laugh.
...we cry.
...we give.
...we take.
...we love.
...we hate.
...we hurt.
...we sin.
...we pray.
...we believe.
...we repent.
...we see.
...we forgive.
...we worship.
...we praise.
...we live.
...we breathe.
...we seek.
...we find...
Jesus.

Black Ink on My Fingers

I look at the black ink on my fingers.
Covered with the ink of my past,
Delivering the news for 20 seasons of my young life,
The days of early mornings sheltered in darkness.
I remember these days as yesterday speeds by,
On rewind in my thought-propelled DVD player.

Images of black ink on my fingers whiz into view.
I stop and remember sweet coffee with cream,
At 1:30 am before the crows begin their morning meeting,
And the roosters make their presence known with shrill greetings,

I let fly the wordy objects from my hands,
And watch them sail on the porch with precision,
While many more follow – Slap! Tap! Slap! Swish!
And they coast into place. Many stairs to climb…
School chimes and I nestle in my seat.
Another day of education in the school building
And on the many street routes.

Black ink settles on the tips of my fingertips.
I let the rubber banded news fly,
Running, moving as fast as I can, so I can finish early,
And treat myself to a corn muffin smothered with jelly,
Accompanied by my sweet coffee with cream,
And relaxing conversation at the breakfast bar.

Black ink spots linger between my finger lines.
I read my current book – the teacher's choice and then,
I read the newsy headlines, a general culmination of various voices,
Telling of the latest news in my big town they call a city.

I sit to do my daily lesson at the table,
Hearing my mother's voice strong, loving, abiding…
Then it's back to the pages of words dancing,
Gliding off my fingers landing in a slide.

Black ink remains in the ridges of my fingerprint.
Track – Slap!
Chorus – Tap!
Violin – Slap!
Traveling – Swish!
Family gatherings, movies, music, team champions –
Slap! Tap! Slap! Swish!
Graduations come and go, and the memories come ablaze in my own news.
My psychological DVD slows and the present whirrs into view.
All grown up now, working, Jesus and career oriented,
Those reminiscences remain fresh, permanently impressed in me.

I press pause on my thoughts and look down at my hands closely.
As I look, as I peer through lines of a piece-of-my-life journey…
I still see the black ink nestled in my fingers.

SAME. DIFFERENCE.

I sat on a pier.
A quiet pier.
Like the parks
I frequented at home.
Parks bright with thistles,
Green trees
And a very dirty pond.

I see the water,
The water – it's different.

Fried dough,
Wafting through the air,
Tickling my nose,
Tickling my memories,
Bringing up a reminiscence:

Of a boardwalk,
Wooden, cut into oval lines,
The edges shaped like ovals.
Fresh wood. Old wood.
It changes because
It's an old memory.

I guess,

The fried dough scent,
Can only reach so far,
Trigger so much.

I see the day,
Brisk wind, walking,
On the shifting wood,

On the sandy beach.
The water rises
Because of the wind.
Overcast, cloudy sky,
But it's still a good day.

I'm drawn
Back to the pier,
To the boats,
The sun shining
Over the waves…
The waves that are still.

It feels the same,
Where I stand,
At the pier.
Not unlike the parks
I frequented at home.

The exception is the water.
The water…that's different.

WALL OF WORDS

Bitterness, unkind words, hectic, volatile reactions:

Brick by brick.

Built up resentments,
Vicious displays of abuse,
Words are the culprit,
But no one sees the:

Brick by brick.

Grabbing the mortar,
Continuing the destruction,
Jealousy, anger, strife…
Rife with exhaustion and pain,
Ugliness of soul,
Non-repentant,
Lacking in Jesus:

And the bricks just keep on comin'…

Life ain't so fantastical
Words not taken back:

Brick by brick.

Laid up in the mortar,
Solidifying the pain,
The drudgery of remorse's enemy,
Desensitization,
Senses dull with pain:

Brick by brick.

Mortar suffocates the sanities,
Still building,
Still trudging,
Still murdering,
With words:

And the bricks just keep on comin'...

'Til the wall is fully constructed –
And you can't see a thing.

TAKING AWAY THE SWISS CHEESE

God causes the light,

To seep through the holes lining

My soul's edges and depths,

Sealing them

From the inside out.

The light breaks through,

Shining through my invisible cavities,

So, I no longer look like swiss cheese.

Now, I walk around like hard cheddar.

QUIET NOISE

Riding in the quiet noise...

Blanketed faces, covered with newspapers,
Books, Magazines, Paperwork,
Anything to keep the eyes averted,
From other sets of eyes straining to stay averted.

Sights and sounds and scenes of buildings,
And trees whiz by, sometimes fast-ly
Sometimes laboriously slow – but still whiz by
Because eyes are blurred, clouded
By tears of aversion.

Music blares within the quiet noise...
Or within the ear drum carried by the iPod,
Or iPhone or whatever instrument
Keeping the lack of comfort zones at bay.

In a seat or standing by a seat –
Avoiding the breath of another or the touch
So unwanted from the all-too-familiar stranger
Standing a hair's breadth away.

Personal space has become a personal phenomenon,
A thing of the past that parents share with their kids,
Describing it as in the days of yore –
A bedtime story to tell the next generation,
Of the great times we used to have
When we had room,

To sit and think in the quiet noise...

Boarding and un-boarding...

Walking on and off the EL...
Standing and sitting...
With averted eyes and space deprivation...

Riding in the quiet noise...
Riding in the quiet noise.

PROCESS *

Overnight syndrome,
Has taken over our societal mores,
From quick fix to quick fix,
A popcorn minute for the microwave generation.

Cyber speed momentum,
With only a moment to recoup,
From a fissure in our sinews, marrow, bones, soul, and spirit,
Sharply searing through regeneration,
Forgetting time takes time to heal.

That Wise Ancient of Days
Provides a Word that notes an old phenomenon:

Process.

From day to day...
From year to year...
From grief to healing...
From loss to acceptance...
From unforgiveness to forgiveness...
From hurt to love...
From anguish to peace...
From *faith to faith...*
From glory to glory.

                         * Romans 1:17 (King James Version)

WISE CHOICE

I can change the world:
With my words!

My praise,
My song,
Any form they fly in.

I can shape my destiny
According to God's plan.
I don't want to make Him
Laugh at me,
But laugh…
With me.

So when I change the world,
I choose His Word!

Then, I guarantee…
We'll be laughing together.

DREAMS

Without dreams inside,
Little cells flowing through me –
Like ice in my veins.

To Be and To Do

Black people just want to be left alone…
To be and to do.

To walk along a pier, up a college staircase,
Jog and make it to our desired destination,
Have a cookout in the park,
Ride a bike,
Protest – with or without arms,
Lift our voices,
Share our pain.
Share our joy.
Be human.

To laugh and to cry.
To sleep and to wake.
To run and to walk.
To work and to play.
To love and to hate.
To be sad and to be happy.
To live and to die.
To talk and to be silent.
To look and to look away.
To flail our arms and to kick our feet.
To dance and to stand still.
To rejoice and to worship.
To feel and to shutter our feelings.
To yell and to whisper.
To be angry and to be excited.
To be emotional and to reflect.
To lead and to listen.
To vote and to debate.
To create and to alter.
To fight and to walk away.

To stand and to sit.
To breathe in and to breathe out.
To breathe.
To be human…

When and where we want to, how we want to, when we choose, God given…God made…*God rights*: They belong to black people…

Nothing to do with some delusional cult that can't let go of a whitewashed, unintelligent, Eurocentric past.

White humans, your color does not take those rights away.

Those with badges of the law who are supposed to protect and serve yet have used them to brutalize and murder and harass and traumatize, do not take those rights away.

White gangs also known as militia and cowardly boys who call themselves men running around in packs, do not take those rights away.

White women who have squawked, bullied, lied, deceived, emitted false tears, and caused the brutal murders of black men, women, and children with each horrific strategy, do not take those rights away.

White inferiority complex, insecurities, unintelligence, hiding behind Christianity, and low self-esteem posed as delusional supremacy, do not take those rights away.

Whites who proactively grandstand or acquiesce in silence to racism, upholding the status quo, do not take those rights away.

Television shrills that thrill in perpetuating racism, do not take those rights away.

Self-hating others who elevate their twisted voices or stew in silence, do not take those rights away.

We are daughters. We are sons.
We are mothers. We are fathers.
We are uncles. We are aunties.
We are grandmothers. We are grandfathers.
We are great grandmothers. We are great grandfathers.
We are children. We are great grandchildren.
We are cousins. We are relatives.
We are godmothers. We are godfathers.
We are young. We are old.
We are men. We are women.
We are generations. We are next generations.
We are creators. We are discerners.
We are people. We are human.
We *are*.

We have *the right* to be left alone...
To be and to do.

So. Leave. Us. Alone.

I'm Not a Poor Frog.

Chapter 8

HEART MADE HAPPY

Well...you've told me
Up on the High tower,
And down the Main street...

You don't like how I bring it.

But you know,
That's alright with me.
'Cause I don't craft this scribe
In search of your deferential esteem,
But for my heart, which likes to flow,
Droppin' a soul-conscious creed,
Keeping it happy along
With those I don't see.

So, I'll just let you be,
What you have become to me:
A sound bite of my word...

For *free*.

Yeah, it may be laced with negativity,
That someone else is bound to see...
But curious from your diatribe of
Steady puttin'-down-me,
Will open my personal ruminations and read...
And read...

And *read*.

And won't it be some kind of
Turned key,
When from your critical seed,

My door of shared reflection is opened…
And in walks
Another heart made happy.

Never Thought

Never thought I'd be out there,
Slippin' into words,
And giving them the rhythm…

A core passion was touched,
The recesses shot up,
And here I am:
Pouring them out to you.

These words that express
My inner being,
Come from an intrusive place.
Whose fire
Seething and climbing,
Blow up at the top
And knock the heaven
Out of my mouth,
Making sure it stays
Open…
To please,
To rattle, to shake,
To cry loud and whisper softly,
To bring contemplation,
A throaty laughter, silent tears, and
Dimpled cheeks,
While giving of myself,
As you watch with curious
Glares, playful stares, and glistening eyes…

Waiting for me to complete
The slippin' out of my soul…
Into yours.

For the Love of Ellipses...

Chapter 9

Relationship...

...requires a bond that is held together by love and the desire to love,
a knowledge of one another that runs deeper than surface reflections,
colloquial and cliché understandings –
that don't require actual learned knowledge.

...requires strength and a willingness to go through overhauls,
changing faces, mood shifts and angry spats,
reconciliation, forgiveness, and love all over again.

...requires endurance and a commitment to endure.
...requires the little things that will keep it all standing together,
the praying, the sweet somethings, the intimate gestures, the sacrifice.

...requires strength and the desire to stand strong.
...requires you and me and not the concept of you and me.
...requires more than one to strive to become one.

...requires a steadfast diligence in allowing God to complete the perfect work
He began when he brought Eve to Adam,
knowing that He is the anchor that keeps it steadfast while strengthening us in our diligence.

...requires enjoyment of that heavenly slice that originated from being *us*.

GRASS IS GRASS (Things aren't always…well you know…)

This place *or*…that place?
Started to walk over to the other side,
Because the grass looked shiny.
It gleamed in the light
Like a beacon of hope –
I thought it was callin' me.

The grass under my feet
Felt a little tough,
Had some brown spots,
Had some wet spots,
Had some wild weeds growing every which-a-way.
Couldn't stand the feel sometimes,
Just got on my ever-livin', lovin', *whatever* nerve in my body.
Just irritated the heck out of me…

Lookin' over at that other grass,
It just looked peaceful,
Just drawin' me.
I couldn't help but walk over.
I craved to feel its smoothness,
'Cause it looked smooth you see.
I just had to have it, had to feel it, had to touch it –
It was callin' me, just callin' my name!

This grass, *oooh*, just got on my nerve!
I just had to get away from it –
Just had to *move on*.
Those brown spots, those wild weeds, those wet spots,
That toughness, the nerve tuggers…

I looked over and I just did it!
I *ran* over to the other side.

To that mowed lawn,
That sweet heaven of well-laid, well-made grass.
When I got there…when I got there…Mm. Mm. Mm…when I got there…!
I just jumped, and let my feet sail right over it!

I opened my eyes and my feet felt so…*burned*!

I looked down and I stared hard.
I could not believe it. I just shook my head…

Mm. Mm. Mm. *Astroturf.*

Peace and Peace's Intermission

Chapter 10

INSIDE PEACE *

Let's break it down:
God given, God nurtured, God infused peace
That *you just don't understand.*
Internally more influential than outside peace.
Well-being…Good being…Love being…You.
A feeling of wholeness through you.
Sweet sleep — drooling and snoring included.
An understanding that you will be alright.
An understanding that *you* are alright.
Regrets unplugged.
Working at having fewer of them regrets.
Patience is a real thing.
Happiness is not a byword.
Contentment is in your bones.
Hope and joy: words you live by.
"Looking forward to…" is not a cliché.
Love is never more than a thought away.
Smiling does not make your reflection look like an alien.
Keeping a dream is just part of your DNA.
Knowing all is well,
Even when it seems like it's not.

* Philippians 4:7 (King James Version)

Quiet.

The sound of a slightly running faucet.
The sound of a refrigerator humming.
The sound of a low turning ceiling fan.
The sound of springs giving in.
The sound of eyelids shuttering.
The sound of a falling eyelash.
The sound of a drumming heartbeat.
The sound of running thoughts slowing to a walk.
The sound of gaited breathing.
The sound of muscles uncoiling.
The sound of a soft cottony imprint.
The sound of a relieved exhale.
The sound of a conversational prayer.
The sound of God's gentle response.
The sound of a contented sigh.
The sound of a soul peace.

Broken Pieces

Broken pieces come in.

They claw, they hurt, they cut deep
At the very essence of you.
They take bit by bit, pieces of your inner man,
Clawing, hurting, cutting deep.

You wish to escape such anguish, such pain.
You wish for a break,
Hoping it will come soon,
Providing you with that necessary relief.

Relief doesn't get rid of the pain though,
Just relieves it a little...
The clawing, the hurting, the cutting deep.

But then comes the revelation of something deeper
Than the broken pieces...
God heals. God delivers. God saves. God sets free...
From the clawing, the hurting, the cutting deep.

My marrow heals...my bones fuse...
My muscle tears mend and redevelop...
My spirit heals...my soul fuses...
My mind mends and redevelops...
Such healing only comes from the Father.
The broken pieces are removed.
The broken pieces are mended together.

When God is finished,
You will never know they were ever broken apart.

Thus ends a saga of the clawing, the hurting, the cutting deep.
I am so relieved.
And in this case...
Just for eternity.

PEACE'S INTERMISSION

Pain is not eternal.
It is temporal.
Though it may *feel* like a small eternity...
It is not *really* eternal.
Selah: *I will pause and think deeply and calmly about that.*

About the Author

W.C. Aldridge uses snapshots of her childhood and a keen sense of faith to weave her experiences and memories through her poetry. She holds a BA in English and an MAED in Curriculum Technology, and worked as a high school teacher and tutor before beginning her freelance writing career in the education field. Since branching out into creative writing, she has written for magazines, created materials for book publishers, and contributed to life stories through ghostwriting. Aldridge currently writes her own column, *Purposeful Gospel Profiles*, which features profiles of gospel artists with a focus on the inspiration behind their music. Aldridge placed 2nd in the 2003 Nubian Poets' Black History Month Contest, was chosen as a finalist for the 2017 Palm Beach Poetry Festival / African American Fellowship and is a 2018 ACT ONE Hollywood Writing Program graduate. She lives in Chicago, Illinois with her husband.

Worldwind Books — Powered by Mind

The Worldwind Books Poetry Series celebrates the power of poetry to reveal and to heal with collected works from diverse contemporary poets. Published in print only, each volume is formatted with spare simplicity and lightly illustrated.

But Who's Counting?
collected poems
by Zelda Leah Gatuskin
ISBN 978-0-938513-41-4

Poetry Night (excerpt)

The first poet
had filled his pockets
with smallish pebbles
which he winged at us hard
Pop Pop Pop Pop
and faster
PopPopPopPopPopPop
and every one hit its mark
We were bruised some
but appreciative

The second poet carried a
notebook full of loose leaves
They fluttered up
when she shuffled them
then drifted gently
down about our heads
. . .

Another Spring
collected poems
by Robin Matthews
ISBN 978-0-938513-50-6

boyhood revisited (excerpt)

maples,
silver & green,
yellow, red,
bare,
masquerading as campfire.

cedar water,
cold,
but irresistible,
astringent as canvas-filtered dawn.

shoulders & backs aching
deliciously of canoes,
we moved,
mysterious as water,
into & out
of summer,

Worldwind Books is an imprint of Amador Publishers, LLC
Albuquerque, New Mexico, USA
www.amadorbooks.com

www.ingramcontent.com/pod-product-compliance
Lightning Source LLC
Chambersburg PA
CBHW071730090426
42738CB00011B/2442